720 Haircuts
Creating Customer Loyalty that Lasts a Lifetime

By
Gary Magenta

Dedication

For the business leaders, managers, and frontline
employees who dedicate their lives to creating,
leading and delivering a great customer experience.

Contents

Acknowledgments

I want to thank my parents, Jon and Karen Magenta, for being great teachers of how to deliver and evaluate a great customer experience. To my uncle, Melvin Druin, for being the inspiration behind *720 Haircuts* and demonstrating what customer loyalty looks like at its best. I have much respect and appreciation for my Root Inc. family's contribution to the research, expertise, feedback, artistry, and assembling of this book. Special thanks go to Shane Beers, Meredith Belman, Phil Hamburg, Angie Hyatt, Erin Kanary, Len Kinor, Heather Lee, Sam Need, JJ Pastore, Aleassa Schambers, Bridget Stallkamp, Dr. Kari Terzino, Anne Urfer, and our partners at Fred Marketing. Thank you for being all that I could hope for in collaborators. To Veronica Hughes, my trusted advisor and partner throughout the writing process; and to Rich Berens, Brad Haudan, and Jim Haudan for being supportive business partners who generously provide me with encouragement and resources to follow my passions. To Margie Heck and Wanda Horn who manage, schedule, and facilitate my work life with care and patience. To my wife, Angela, and my children, Ian and Jordan, who have allowed me the time and space to dedicate myself to writing a second book. I know *720 Haircuts* came to be at the expense of our time spent together. I am both grateful and apologetic.

Foreword

Culture is no longer a buzzword used in boardrooms. It has real implications across every organization in every industry. What separates one culture from another is the passion behind it and how it translates to brand and customer experience.

It's culture that can help your brand rise above the noise, to stand out in a sea of sameness. Culture is what will allow you to rise above competitors and stake your claim as an industry leader. The importance of differentiating from the competition is not unique to our industry. It's a reality every company has to navigate. At Hampton, we never stop being mindful of this opportunity. Keeping our product fresh and relevant to the ever-changing needs of our guests is the ante to the game. Building and inspiring a strengths-based culture is what wins the hand. It is our culture that enables us to perpetuate our founder Conrad Hilton's vision "to fill the earth with the light and warmth of hospitality." It is this vision that drives us all at Hampton to stand out through a carefully cultivated culture (or through the culture we have so carefully cultivated.)

Let's be honest, the minute you roll out innovative changes to your products and services, your competitors are only a few steps behind you. (Not in a creepy stalkerish way, but they're watching… and imitation is the sincerest form of flattery, right?)

Here's the thing. While anyone can implement aesthetic changes like curved shower rods and washable duvet covers in hotel rooms, they can't replicate your culture. And that's why it's crucial to invest in your people. At Hampton, our culture is our customer experience. 'Hamptonality' – as we call it – bleeds into every facet of our business. It starts with our leaders, trickles down to our team members and franchisees, and then results in an authentic customer experience that just can't be duplicated. That's our secret sauce.

It's also the crux of Gary Magenta's, *720 Haircuts*. He hammers the point home (over and over again) about why it's so critical to create differentiated customer experiences. This notion applies to every industry and should be on the radar of every company leader in regard to standing apart from competition. If you're reading this book, it must be on your radar, so… good for you.

Gary's ideas about empowering managers and frontline employees, and creating authenticity at every touch point, are key to separating yourself from the pack. He reminds us of an important lesson that should never be swept under the rug – your products and services alone will not determine your success, your people will.

The best thing you can do is to create a culture of owners by giving them the tools and the confidence to act like your business is their business. We know from our own re-invention that this happens when you invest in your people and empower them to create the customer experience you want to represent your brand. Hamptonality wasn't just a fun word. It was a revolution with its own persona. Hamptonality would set the tone for the future of our brand, serving as the cornerstone of how we would engage our people across a whole network of franchised locations - more than 2100 hotels in 20 countries, and growing.

At the heart of any customer-focused brand is exactly that – engagement. It's another topic Gary touches on in this book, and for good reason. Engagement begets engagement. Gary's perspective underscores the importance of focusing on and investing in your people as the engine for customer experience change. When your people are engaged to deliver on your customer experience vision, you have the power to turn customers into true evangelists. That's what makes all the difference in success over the long term.

In *720 Haircuts*, Gary teaches us an important lesson about why we need to invest time, energy and resources in our people. You can mimic the innovations we make to our guest rooms, you can even duplicate the artwork hanging on our walls - but you simply cannot replicate our people and our culture and the power it has on our customer experiences. Our people are ultimately the ones who make our customers come back again and again and again. What's more important than that?

Gina Valenti
Hilton Worldwide
Vice President – Brand Hospitality, Midscale Brands

Preface

What if all your customers fell in love with your business and the experience that you created for them?

What if their love was so deep they would pay more, drive farther, and literally step over your competition to get to you?

What if your customers shopped with you with their emotions as well as their wallets?

My Uncle Mel has done just that. For the last 60 years, from age 14 to 74, he has visited the same establishment, without fail, to have his hair cut. The location has changed several times. The employees have morphed over the years. But no matter where he's lived, from a few blocks away to over a 100-mile round trip, he has been unwavering in his loyalty. Twelve haircuts a year for 60 years … that's *720 haircuts* – and counting!

Why is that? And how can *you* generate that type of loyalty to *your* business?

In this book, we'll talk about the kind of customer experience that inspires loyalty like this. For some organizations, it's almost second nature. For others, it's elusive. Over the years, I've learned from some of the best companies that there are simple yet essential elements to inspiring loyalty. We'll explore the vital roles of leaders, managers, and the frontline as they work together to deliver a great customer experience. Together, everyone in your business is responsible for building a culture, acting like owners, and crafting authentic experiences.

Through stories, case studies, and real-life examples, you'll uncover the secrets to creating customers who are loyal to your business for life.

Chapter 1
The Making of a Customer Experience Revolutionary

Whether your customers are waiting in a line, ordering online, squeezing a dime or splurging in an upscale restaurant, if you can't create an emotional connection between your business and your customer, you're in serious trouble! The only true competitive advantage your business has, in this omni-channel and consumer-centric world, is a differentiated customer experience.

I've been a lifelong student of the customer experience.

Some of my earliest childhood memories are about shopping with my mother in Pompton Lakes, New Jersey, during the 1960s. That town was – and still is – a middle-class blue-collar community with a main street filled with stores that weren't particularly fancy but met the needs of the local consumers. When I was growing up, we had a typical mix of retailers. There was a fish market, a small independent grocery, a flower shop, a beauty salon, a pharmacy, a pizza parlor, a butcher shop, and a haberdashery. We had a shoe store, a gas station, a bank, a movie theatre – the Colonial, where I once enjoyed a *Planet of the Apes* marathon – and even an S&H Green Stamps redemption center where thrifty moms would trade stamps earned from purchases for tray tables, small appliances, and other cool stuff.

My mother was always working, but she also seemed to always be shopping, with me in tow in both instances. I remember how those shopping trips unfolded:

"Good morning, Mrs. Magenta! How was the fillet of sole last week? Did you prepare it the way I suggested?"

"Hi, Mrs. Magenta! Gary must be ready to start kindergarten. Let's go to the Husky department so we can find him some new school clothes."

"Mrs. Magenta, I have some sample centerpieces for you to choose from for that PTA fundraiser. Let me show you what I've come up with."

Whatever the store, she could always count on this: The owners were there to greet her, they knew her name, they knew her preferences, and they were ready to advise and guide her in making the right selections. It was a personal, authentic experience. Even though my mom was only in her twenties, she was always welcomed with respect and catered to by all the local merchants, who knew our family, our needs, and our likes and dislikes.

The Customer is Always Right... Even When They're Wrong

My parents' business was like this, too. Together, they designed, manufactured, and sold uniforms for police, firefighters, and postal workers. The retail part of their business had been established by my grandparents in the 1940s, so my father had grown up in it before taking it over in the 1960s.

There was nothing about the uniform business and its customers that my father didn't know. He and my grandfather had clothed generations of police and firefighters. He knew every uniform of every police and fire department in the state of New Jersey and parts of New York and Pennsylvania. He knew each customer by name and rank, and he knew their past purchases. I'd hear them say to my dad:

> "Jon, your father sold me my first uniform when I graduated from the police academy, and now I'm about to retire! Where did the time go?"

> "Jon, what's the color of the new shirt my department specified? I can't remember."

> "Jon, what's the best bullet-proof vest on the market today?"

Even as a kid, I could see what great customer service looked like and how it was delivered.

My father was indeed a trusted advisor and an expert for all of his customers. Like the shopkeepers my mother visited, he knew his customers' names, needs, wants, and preferences. He welcomed customers into his business as if they were friends. Like his own father, he offered them a shopping experience that was personal and authentic, and they liked it. He modeled that behavior for all the salespeople who worked with his customers. You could see my grandfather's philosophy come to life in my father and all his sales associates – including me. That philosophy was "The customer is always right – even when they're wrong."

So, even as a little kid, I was privy to what great customer service looked like to a consumer and how a shopkeeper should deliver it. I developed a unique viewpoint on how it felt to be treated as a valued customer, and also the nuances between bad, good, and great customer service.

I started half-day kindergarten in 1967 when I was four. My mom picked me up every day at noon and took me back to our family business, where I spent the rest of the day. Before long, I was given small jobs – at first, sweeping up scraps of material dropped by the garment cutters and seamstresses. Later, I helped in shipping and receiving, unpacking boxes and stocking inventory. I learned to operate the sewing and cutting machines. By the time I was 13, I was waiting on customers in our family's retail store – the same ones my grandfather and father had served before me.

I was a natural at it. I enjoyed the interactions – hearing stories and telling them, asking questions to learn customers' needs and wants, and solving problems. Most of all, I enjoyed getting to know those people. I was also able to be my absolute authentic self as I simultaneously satisfied clients and delivered great customer service. It was very gratifying. I didn't know that customer service was a "thing," but I was already doing it.

The Two-Job Teenager

At closing time, I went directly to my second job as a busboy and later a waiter in a local catering house. So before 5:15 pm, I served customers who wanted uniforms to put *on* their bodies, and after 5:15, I served customers who wanted food to put *in* their bodies. Both of these are very personal. Both involve customers with very specific needs, desires, and expectations. My role was to satisfy them all. You may think this was a stressful adolescence. You'd be wrong. I loved working and serving all kinds of customers.

Working up to six days a week at two jobs, I made some decent money. I even had my own checkbook, and retailers didn't see many teenagers who wrote checks. Although I spent quite a bit for someone my age, clerks didn't take me all that seriously, and they didn't pay me much attention. Even then, I knew the customer service I was receiving was a far cry from what I was delivering in my own two jobs. I was still a teenager, but I started seeking out establishments that provided better customer service.

Now, this was the late 1970s. "Main Street" was dying. Chain stores in malls were proliferating. In just a decade, the shopping experience had changed dramatically. Remember, I had witnessed the behavior of one of the world's greatest shoppers (my mother) as well as a world-class deliverer of great customer service (my dad). I learned what I should expect as a consumer. I also began to understand the real meaning of customer service and noticing something even more meaningful: the overall customer experience. "Customer service" is something that happens during a single purchase, but "customer experience" is bigger. It's every interaction with that business – in person, on the phone, and through technology. The customer experience is what shapes the emotional tie to a product or service.

> I knew the customer service I was receiving was a far cry from what I was delivering in my own two jobs.

I was looking for that connection. (We'll talk more about this difference in upcoming chapters.)

The bar was set very high. I expected a lot – as should all customers. From that point on, I searched for and shopped at places that fulfilled my idea of delivering great customer service *and* overall great customer experience. Although I didn't know it at the time, I was on my way to becoming a true Customer Experience Revolutionary.

Welcome to the Revolution – Again

Actually, there have always been customer revolutions. Throughout history, customers have driven merchants to change their products and services in response to their own evolving lifestyles and needs. Customers demand,

and businesses respond. And it's not just what they sell, but *how* they sell – from traders to peddlers to Main Street shopkeepers to chain stores to big-box giants. And now, changes that once took centuries are happening in years or months, and sometimes even overnight.

Today, a new revolution has erupted specifically in the world of customer experience, and it's possibly the biggest shift in consumer behavior we've seen in decades. It's kind of a big deal, and probably important to you because you're reading this book. We're seeing a fundamental, dynamic change in what consumers expect from businesses across industries.

A revolution has erupted in the world of customer experience.

Consumers are leading a popular and swift movement in which they reward businesses who meet their demands with their loyalty. These "Consumer Revolutionaries" now expect and even *demand* an overhaul in the way businesses engage with them. Those who ignore them will be left behind – battered, bruised, and in some cases, lying in the Graveyard of Failed Businesses.

In response to this revolution, many businesses have already heavily invested in creating a unique customer experience by focusing on processes and technology, the "stuff" that keeps a business running. All of this is very important, and it totally supports the customer experience. If you've already done this, congratulations! You've arrived at the halfway mark.

But what about the need to create an *emotional connection* between your customers and your brand? Creating that emotional connection is the true determinant of customer loyalty. It is your company's fingerprint, individual to you and your business.

Creating an emotional connection is the true determinant of customer loyalty.

In this book, we'll uncover the secrets about customer loyalty and making the emotional connections that help create that loyalty. This is what has people talking about you, paying more for your products or services, and walking past your competition to get to you. In other words, that emotional connection you make is where customer loyalty lives.

My promise to you is this: By the time you finish reading this book, you'll have a simple yet effective framework for creating loyal customers for your business.

TRY THIS

- Identify your target customer.
- Determine your core offering to that customer.
- Ask your customers about their current emotional connection to your product or service.
- Determine the most important emotional connection you'd like to make with your customers.

NOTES

NOTES

Chapter 2
The Customer Experience Revolution: We've All Been "Starbuckized"

To understand the importance of the customer experience today, we need to take a deeper look at the past.

During the first half of the 20th century, retailers focused on creating loyal customers by establishing an emotional connection. In a bricks-and-mortar store, this was done face-to-face, but it was quite possible to do it another way – through mail order, the ancestor of online shopping.

One of the best examples of a company that built an emotional connection to its brand was Sears and Roebuck, originally a mail-order business. You could order just about anything from the Sears catalog, from clothing to housewares to farm tools. (Does this sound familiar, Amazon shoppers?)

And as for an emotional connection? Well, when the Sears catalog arrived in the mail, that was a good day! For most people, rural or not, this was their basic link to the latest trends, their window into everything from the current fashions to technological advancements. It was literally a "mall in a mailbox." No matter your age, geographic location, or economic status, that catalog bonded people – farmers with bankers, generations of all ages, and faraway friends. Everybody loved it. And they remained loyal customers for life.

Up through the 1950s, women who worked in the home were called "housewives" or "homemakers," and they made an art form of running a household and managing a family. Those were the days when people actually changed drapes in the spring and fall, when there was a difference between "play clothes" and "school clothes." Moms stayed home to manage the house and family, dads worked from 9 to 5 without ridiculous extra hours or weekend travel, and going out to eat was for special occasions only.

For the most part when people shopped in stores, it wasn't for fun; it was for a purpose. "Retail therapy" wasn't for the masses. During the Great Depression and World War II, people had learned to be frugal. The average family had a budget. Mom carefully planned a weekly menu and visited the grocery store just once a week. She shopped at an independent market where the owner knew her name, gave recommendations, and likely checked her out and bagged her groceries. People shopped for clothing for a season at a time – the four seasons being winter, spring, summer, and "school." And shopkeepers delivered a quality customer experience with a personal touch.

The satisfying customer experience of those early years all but disappeared during the social upheaval of the 1960s and '70s. The 1960s had been a sort of boom time economically, but the 1970s took a financial U-turn. Prices went up, commodities went down, and no one's salary was increasing. Women left their aprons in the kitchen and joined the workforce to add to the family income – but they were still running their households, resulting in a huge time crunch. A dual-earner household required speed and in-the-moment convenience. Mothers, and now dads, became over-scheduled and

needed to get more done in less time at a lower cost.
At the same time, the Women's Liberation Movement was in full swing. Following the fight for civil rights, women were stepping up to claim an equal place in businesses. Nearly every advertisement for women's products highlighted this, from Virginia Slims cigarettes' slogan, "You've Come a Long Way, Baby," to Enjoli perfume, whose theme song included the lyrics, "I can bring home the bacon, fry it up in a pan, and never let you forget you're a man." Helen Reddy's #1 hit song of 1972, "I Am Woman," became the *de facto* anthem for millions of women who were striving to expand their horizons past the white picket fence.

So no matter what the reasons – economic need, convenience, time crunch, empowerment, or all of the above – the world was changing. These unprecedented shifts in marketplace forces required an unprecedented response from the business world. Women were entering the workforce just as the economy was turning sour. The convenience needs of the American family soared, and businesses saw the economies of scale and greater levels of profitability that could be reached with new store formats and in different shopping venues.

Changes in the Game of Retail

Those downtown stores that opened at 9 and closed at 5 eventually went out of business. Giant shopping malls started popping up everywhere. They housed multiple shoe stores, department stores, jewelry boutiques, and bookstores, where consumers could compare similar products before deciding what to purchase.

Consumers were shopping in a new way, and retailers were staffing to meet the changing needs. To offer what consumers now demanded – speed, convenience, and low prices – retailers no longer hired "career shopkeepers" who took pride in sharing their expertise, being a trusted advisor who spent time with each customer. Instead, they hired hourly workers who were simply seeking a paycheck. Hourly employees weren't required to be enthusiastic or knowledgeable about what they were selling. They were warm bodies who were merely expected to efficiently process a customer and move on to the next person in line.

The average consumer wasn't expecting personal service at this time. The rules were different.

This sounds harsh, but to be fair to businesses, the average consumer wasn't demanding or even *expecting* personal service at this time. They knew this was the tradeoff for lower prices and convenience. Consumer priorities had changed. The rules were different.

Mass retailing still needed to learn to be deliberate in delivering a customer experience. Retailers were focused on opening stores, bringing in merchandise, and keeping up with competitors' inventory and pricing. They weren't intentionally doing the wrong thing; they were just meeting the expressed needs of their customers at that time. American sociologist George Ritzer says that companies adopted a process that followed four criteria – predictability, efficiency, calculability, and control. But that left out people and emotions.[1]

Throughout the 1980s and '90s, retailers focused on products and services as the sole differentiators between them and their competitors. But as we know, even the best products and services can be knocked off.

It's Not Just About the Tapas

If you've been to Spain, you know about tapas bars. Legend has it that their origins began in the 10th century when one tavern owner served wine in a glass and added a piece of bread to keep flies from dropping into the wine. People liked the added touch. His competitor down the street not only stole the idea, but added his own upgrade: a piece of cheese atop the bread. Not to be outdone, another competitor placed an olive on the cheese that topped the bread. In time, an entirely new style of food was developed, all in an effort to differentiate one tavern from the rest.

While I'm pleased that tapas came about because I love them, the real differentiator was never solely the tapas. It was the combination of the tapas and the *experience* that

[1]Ritzer, George (2006). *McDonaldization: The Reader.* Thousand Oaks, CA: Pine Forge Press.

the bartender delivered. People want to eat, drink, and have fun – and it's that emotional connection of great food, great wine and a fun bartender that makes them choose one bar over another.

Like the tapas bars, each store in the new malls tried to distinguish itself from its competitors. Retailers and service providers had to learn that it wasn't just about the tapas. Their products and services were *not* the sole determinants of satisfaction. Those things were just cheese on bread; what consumers were really looking for was an emotional connection – products and services they wanted, delivered by someone they enjoyed talking to.

An emotional connection – that key component of the customer experience – is something that can't be knocked off or duplicated. Creating it and having the ability to deliver it consistently is the Holy Grail. It's the top thing consumers yearn for and the number-one indicator of success.

The most progressive businesses create an emotional connection with customers as their competitive edge.

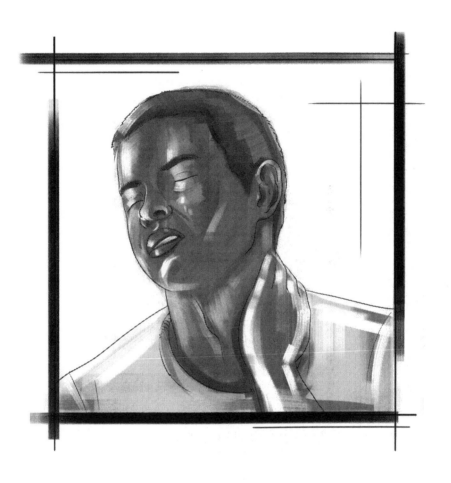

Customer Experience Whiplash

So what's the rallying cry of this latest retail revolution? *Consumers want it all!* They want to have the same individualized shopping experience of Main Street of the 1950s and '60s with the convenience and competitive pricing of the '70s and '80s. As businesses were one-upping each other on products, services, warranties, and even quality, the most progressive ones started investing in creating an emotional connection with consumers as the clear differentiator. In essence, they were combining the best of both worlds. These progressive businesses realized that *great products and a great experience were equally as important* and they went about creating a customer experience commensurate with their product.

Some companies "got it" from the start. Retailers like Nordstrom – even after 100-plus years in business – created a new level of customer experience. The ultra-personal services spoiled shoppers and made other stores seem embarrassingly backward. Nordstrom became the gold standard, and people began to expect that same type of experience elsewhere. When they didn't get it, they became upset, disappointed, and eventually disloyal. Consumers were left to wonder, "Why can't I get that same experience everywhere I spend my money?" Indeed.

Compare that Nordstrom experience to this – a scenario we're all familiar with:

- You arrive home from your favorite store, pleased with your customer experience.

- You then find your utility bill in the mail, and when

you open it, you discover an error.

- You call the company and are connected to a menu of choices requiring you to press numbers.

- Those numbers lead to other instructions and eventually to a promise to be connected to a live person.

- When you finally reach that live representative, he tells you he can't help you and needs to transfer you to someone else: "Hold, please."

You've just experienced a bad but common case of customer experience whiplash!

Consumers expect – and *should* expect – a great customer experience from every product and service provider they deal with.

Starbuckization
One of the best examples of a company that creates an emotional connection with customers is Starbucks, where baristas write your name on your cup so you feel recognized and so they can remember your name and special drink the next time you come in. In a way, we've all been "Starbuckized." We want personal service and we want it customized to us. We have high expectations.

Places like Whole Foods and Trader Joe's hire people who not only know all about the products they sell but also have the skills to engage with customers authentically. These new workers know the merchandise thoroughly and remember regular customers' needs and preferences so they can recommend products with expertise and personalization. Here, retailers are making an emotional connection and delivering a great customer experience!

And this goes even further. Some companies appeal to customers who buy based on a company's special purpose – those who work to save the environment or benefit people in need. Shopping with these companies adds to the customer experience, making consumers part of something bigger and adding to the loyalty factor.

We've all been "Starbuckized." We want personal service in a customized atmosphere.

We all want that special experience when we shop, no matter how and no matter whom we're dealing with. The best companies are learning to deliver a product or service in a way that makes customers smile – not cringe. Customers want their experience to be consistent, not just within a store, but across the entire brand. We're not just talking about luxury brands. Even bargain shoppers are looking for a special experience.

Yes, we've been "Starbuckized," but we're willing to spend more and travel farther to have the customer experience we desire. So, the pressure's really on the businesses we consider patronizing to get us, make it personal, and keep us. We want to be connected.

TRY THIS

- Identify the areas in your customer experience that can be personalized to customers today.
- Determine opportunities where you can provide an even greater level of personalization than you offer today.
- With your team, brainstorm ways to personalize the customer experience online as well as in face-to-face situations.
- Consider how you can differentiate your business from your competitors' businesses through personalization and customization.

NOTES

NOTES

Chapter 3
Customer Service vs.
the Customer Experience

When was the last time you walked into a store completely in the dark about the product or service you wanted to buy, knowing nothing about its features or benefits? Or pricing? Or manufacturers' reviews? Or competitive offerings in the marketplace? If you're anything like today's average savvy shopper, you've done your homework – probably online – long before you leave home.

In the past, you may have relied on a sales associate, a true expert, for the same information you're getting on your computer today. You built a relationship with a sales associate as he or she educated you and engaged you in your wants, needs, desires, and expectations of the products and services they offered. In the end, you made a decision based on that relationship. You might have thought, "Both of those companies offer a similar product, but I really like Joey," so you bought from Joey. But in today's world, *a lot fewer people are talking to Joey.* In fact, there are a lot fewer Joeys – true experts. Customer service is no less important; it's just consumed in more and different ways. And the information we provide customers is no less important; we just need to replicate "Joey" and the service he provides in an online format.

Let's look at the statistics to highlight this consumer shift. In yesterday's world, 70% of a shopper's decision to buy was based on the influence of salesperson, and 30% was based on research or a recommendation from a friend. Today, those numbers have flipped – 70% of consumers have already decided what they're going to buy and where they're going to buy it based on their own research on the web and recommendations from social media *before they ever interact with a salesperson or customer service rep.* This means you can directly influence only 30% of prospective buyers.

70% of consumers decide what they're going to buy based on their own research.

So when you have a chance to offer customer service, it can clearly make a big difference. The term "customer service" has been around ever since vendors sold their wares from pushcarts in the streets, but "customer experience" is a more recent term. What's the difference? Quite a bit. While *where* and *how* people experience customer service has changed, all consumers are judging the overall customer experience they have when dealing with your business.

Let's look at the distinctions and connections between customer service and customer experience.

> **"Customer service"** takes place during a single transaction between a consumer and a merchant. It's the interaction your business has with a customer at a single moment or touchpoint.

"Customer experience," on the other hand, is the interaction your business has with customers during every touchpoint that spans the entire shopping relationship. Consumers measure their overall customer experience by considering how well every touchpoint measures up to their expectations. All those touchpoints combine to build relationships that make people want to return and inspire them to promote your business to others.

Customer experience is the interaction your business has with customers during every touchpoint.

Customer service is actually an important part of the customer experience. Each touchpoint is an opportunity to gain or lose in the Game of Trust. Those interactions are becoming increasingly less frequent for today's consumers. So businesses looking to succeed must think about expanding past the idea of just delivering great customer service.

Most business leaders – with the best of intentions – have a laser-like focus on creating processes, procedures, and protocols that deliver a differentiated and superior customer experience at many customer touchpoints. But in reality, more than half of any customer experience is created and evaluated based on feelings and emotions.

The customer experience is judged by the *heart* of the consumer, not the *head*. If the goal is loyalty, businesses must consider all of the touchpoints that drive that loyalty. The customer experience – good, bad, or indifferent – is created when these touchpoints are brought to life by the people on your front lines – those who engage with your customer electronically, in person, or both. It's up to them to create an emotional connection whenever possible.

Your ability to set your customer experience above and beyond the competition depends on how well your employees consistently deliver at each of those touchpoints. Organizations spend thousands (and, in some cases, millions) of dollars every day to create consciousness of a brand, product, or service in an effort to acquire those elusive new customers and gain their loyalty. All of those efforts can be supported or destroyed in seconds through a simple interaction with a person or technology.

Depending on how the business treats them, customers will walk away with one of these feelings:
- "Delighted" – I want to come back!
- "Detached" – I'm not delighted…but I'm not disgruntled either.
- "Dissatisfied" – I won't return.

Buying Insurance – Once at Your Kitchen Table, Now on Your iPhone

Here's a story of one company's desire to keep its customer experience the same, and its *customers'* desire to have that customer experience delivered in a new way.

I recently worked with a small insurance company that took great pride in what it called its "world-class customer service." For more than a hundred years, leaders saw this as the company's greatest competitive advantage – the very foundation of the organization. Employees sold insurance not in an office, but in their customers' *homes*, creating trusted "family" relationships that lasted for decades. Any insurance company could have skillfully sold the product, but this company provided a level of personalized expertise – a great customer experience – that was passed on from one generation to the next.

But leaders and employees began realizing that the world was changing, and with it, the way people were buying things – including insurance. Today's customer no longer wants an agent to sit down at their kitchen table a few times a year and explain new details in their policies, and they don't want to call someone to get their account information, even if it is a trusted advisor they've known for years. Today's customers want full access and transparency at their fingertips – online, anytime.

So was this the end of this company's stronghold in delivering personalized customer service? Did the next generation of customers want a great customer experience?

Of course they didn't. They just wanted it delivered differently.

As clear as this message seemed to be, some employees staunchly stuck to the belief that what had worked for the last hundred years would continue to work in the present. They saw no other way to hold on to their primary point of pride – customer service delivered through *an emotional connection specifically delivered through in-person interaction.* In fact, the live interaction actually formed a dependency, as customers had limited access to their policy information without speaking to their salesperson or customer service agent.

But the time came when the company could no longer ignore the banging of the drums of customers and competitors who had, seemingly overnight, changed the rules of the insurance game. Leaders embarked on an organizational transformation to make sure their long-standing service promise continued without interruption, but was delivered in the way customers desired. This business was built on personal relationships, and that would not/should not/could not change. Leaders had to figure out how to maintain those emotional connections, and now, at least in part, through technology.

Success for this company, *as determined by its customers,* required leaders to quickly get on the same page in the form of a total customer experience. They needed to make sure that everyone in the business understood what this new customer experience looked like, which key touchpoints actually determined customer loyalty, and how they would deliver that experience along the customer journey.

When I first met the leaders of this company, they had begrudgingly embarked on the technological shift. I say "begrudgingly" because they saw this shift as a necessary evil, and weren't thinking about the potential benefits. The development of their proprietary technology was relegated to the basement, to be built in isolation. It was if they were almost apologizing for creating it! Their employees were not only in the dark about what was being built for them, but they were petrified about the change.

The company desperately needed a way to transform the mindset, actions, and behaviors of their business and employees. And up to this point, everyone was in the dark. Together, we outlined a plan that would help transform the customer experience, the way it was delivered and the company itself. This plan included three major initiatives:

1. Align leaders – Ensure leaders are on the same page:
  • Gather customer and employee insights to inform the strategy for change.
  • Design a new customer experience that includes all customer service touchpoints of yesterday but offers them in multiple ways.
  • Create a roadmap for employees showing how the company would move from where they are today to where they want to be tomorrow.

2. **Deploy – Engage everyone in the company to "get in the game":**
   - Fortify managers at every level, helping them build skills to lead the new customer experience strategy and keep it alive.
   - Involve employees at every level in *why* things are changing, what was changing, and how *each person* needed to change specifically to deliver the new customer experience.

3. **Sustain – Invest in people:**
   - Train frontline people on each touchpoint, technological and those that include human interaction, to deliver the customer experience in a way that meets consumers' changing needs.

The leadership team embarked on a mission to define the new customer experience journey in its entirety, which included redesigning every customer service touchpoint. We poured through the existing customer experience data to understand what the customer valued most. We held several alignment sessions with the leadership team, which still included a family member of the original founder. As my team started our work with this client, we knew the change ahead was a big one for the leaders and employees. It became clear that the impending systems and technology evolution would require an upgrade of epic proportions. This is where I'd like to tell you that my team helped this company to successfully develop a customer experience strategy, re-define each customer service touchpoint, and engage all employees. I'd like to tell you that all of this happened and that everyone lived happily ever after. But, I can't.

In the middle of the first stage of our transformation process, the CEO of the company accepted an offer from a larger insurance company to purchase the business. Selling a 100-year-old business that was still being led by the same family member could not have been an easy decision to make. Was the change too overwhelming? Was there a lack of confidence in a positive outcome? Was the offer just too good to pass up? In the end, the decision was made based on a belief that the company's legacy of delivering great customer service would be better served by the systems and technology that the new owner could offer, and that it could be done quickly. The customer service the company prided itself on could flourish and be delivered through the same trusted advisors – and the customers' overall experience would be elevated with access to new systems and technology. The access and immediacy to these tools and processes could quickly translate its greatest capability – customer service – into both human *and* technological touchpoints that would create a great customer experience relevant for today's buyer.

This company went on a journey to deliver a great customer experience in a fast evolving marketplace with changing demands. Ultimately, its leaders recognized the reality of the speed of change and just how far behind they were. They made a decision that ensured customers would get the experience they needed and wanted quickly and effectively.

When it comes to customer experience, sometimes you have to make really tough decisions. It doesn't matter if your business is all online or all in-person or a combination of the two. Considering the customer experience in its totality is key, and adjusting to changing customer needs quickly will set you apart from your competitors. Don't fall into the trap of focusing only on specific customer service touchpoints, you could lose sight of the forest through the trees. Concentrate on the *emotions* created in the overall customer experience – the culmination of all the customer service touchpoints. Make sure you are delivering that experience in a way that is relevant to the customer, in-person and through technology. Be prepared to make decisions that aren't easy or comfortable for you and your employees to keep up with changing consumer needs and wants. Decisions made with these as the first priority result in customers who are delighted, want to come back, and become loyal.

TRY THIS

- Identify all the customer service touchpoints in your business, human and through technology.
- Identify service objectives at each touchpoint from the customer's point of view.
- Determine the emotions you want your customer to feel at each touchpoint.
- Identify what decisions need to be made within the delivery of specific touchpoints to create an overall experience that matches your customers changing needs and wants.

NOTES

NOTES

Chapter 4
Online Is the New Frontline

When I was a kid, one of my favorite movies was Woody Allen's 1973 film, *Sleeper*, co-starring his then-girlfriend, Diane Keaton. The story chronicles the adventures of a jazz musician and owner of a health food store who had been cryopreserved (frozen) for 200 years and is defrosted in the year 2173. He awakens in a very different world from the one he had left. Health nuts now eat red meat (Atkins?), and robots perform household chores (Roomba?). The robots are not limited to domestic duties; there are also retail-robots. When Woody Allen's character, Miles, needs to be outfitted for a suit, he's taken to Ginsberg & Cohen's Computerized Fittings, where two tailor-robots take computerized measurements of their new customer and instantly manufacture a suit for him, which is dispensed vending-style.

Miles didn't have to do anything in advance. He just walked into a retail store void of any humans – and yet, *he got a customer experience.* There were touchpoints from being greeted as he entered through the "personalization" of his garments. The frontline of Ginsberg & Cohen was made up of computerized robots. And believe me when I tell you, they delivered an *experience.*

I'm not predicting robots taking the place of humans in stores. I am, however, suggesting that "online is the new frontline" and that your existing frontline and its composition will dramatically change in the coming years, if you haven't noticed it beginning to happen already.

All the basic information about your products, services, and processes can already be handled without a human frontline associate. Price, quality, availability, and selection no longer require the assistance of a frontline employee. However, if your customer does need to speak to a live employee, it's because their needs are complex or they have a problem. These are conversations once handled only by a manager or someone with more responsibility or expertise. Finding the cheapest "disposable" talent won't cut it for the new frontline. The customer's next interaction must be with an expert — a "nexpert" — who can actually solve their problem. Ensuring that your new frontline (online) meets as many of your customers' needs as possible is paramount to success.

Your existing frontline will dramatically change in the coming years.

Designing for Invisible Customers Doesn't Work

While working with a client in the airline business, I had mentioned that their website and application developers, as well as programmers, should take part in the customer experience learning and training we were conducting. His reply was a little surprising to me: "Why would they take customer experience training? They sit in the dark, programming all day. They've never even *seen* a passenger."

Hmm…they've never seen a passenger, but they spend their days developing and programing for millions, literally tens of millions, of passenger transactions? I found that curious.

Finding the cheapest "disposable" talent won't cut it for the new frontline.

Just a few years back, these same passengers would have called a reservation desk to get information and make travel plans, and then gone to an agent to check in for their flights. Those agents would have "known" the customer intimately, and they would have been invested in some form of customer experience training, right? Or at least customer service training? Now that the majority of passengers make their reservations and check in for their flights online, don't they still expect a great experience? Sure they do! Is it possible that people who develop and program online customer experiences don't need to know the customer? Is it possible that they don't need customer experience training? The hell they don't!

I travel extensively for work, and it's not unusual for me to use several airlines in the same week. One day, I was checking in for a flight with Airline A at an airport kiosk. Check-in was intuitive and speedy – a great experience. The following day, I checked in at an airport kiosk with Airline B. I thought, "Am I crazy, or does the wheel on this computer screen keep spinning and spinning? Why is it taking so long? Is the machine broken?" I hit the restart button and found that it wasn't broken at all, but the "think time" that the computer needed was considerably longer with Airline B than Airline A. I did some research later and was able to verify that there was a full 30 seconds' difference between kiosk check-in on these two airlines! Is 30 seconds really a big deal? If you're a busy traveler with a cell phone in one hand, a briefcase in the other and luggage to carry, racing to go to another appointment, it's a huge deal. It's a huge deal to the mom or dad with two kids tugging on their arms, or to the nervous first-time traveler.

It's imperative to train the creators of the online experience just like any other frontline employee.

So do the developers of the kiosk check-in system of Airline B know what the customer experience is like?

Have they stood in the shoes of their competitors? Do they know the impact of 30 seconds on that touchpoint and how it can make or break that customer experience? They should!

Consider this: There has been a seismic shift now that customers can learn about your company and even make their first purchase from your company online. This means that, from the very start, their experience has to be flawless and have a competitive edge. Therefore, it's imperative to train the creators of the online experience just as you would any other frontline employee.

Blockbuster's Fatal Mistake

"People are always going to want to come to us for movies and games. They want the store experience and the guidance and recommendations of an associate. Netflix poses no a threat to us."

Those are the words that I heard at Blockbuster's headquarters in 2001. The company's executives were getting a lot of flak from investors, and even customers, for turning down the chance to buy the still-struggling Netflix for a mere $50 million in 2000. At the time, Blockbuster was the leading provider of home movie and video games through their retail store-based rental services. At its peak, in 2004, Blockbuster had 60,000 employees and 9,000 stores. Then, Netflix had a subscription-based business model that allowed customers to select their movies and games online, get their products in the mail, and return them in a provided envelope.

No stores, no customer experience, no checkout lines splashed with candy and popcorn. Netflix offered many of the same products and convenience – a differentiated experience online.

If we fast-forward a few years, we find Blockbuster delisted from the New York Stock Exchange in 2010. As of 2015 Blockbuster had only 51 remaining stores in the United States. At the same time Netflix was trading at around $115 per share. While still in the subscription business, they progressed into the on-demand streaming media business with $5.5 billion in revenue in 2014 and 69 million subscribers.

Blockbuster's idea of delivering the customer experience – being the trusted advisor – was very rooted in their physical space, the retail stores. They believed that their customers wanted to have an "experience" when they rented a movie or game. I believe they were 100% right – their customers *did* want to have an experience, but it didn't have to be in a store. Blockbuster's leaders were so focused on the retail space and the physical in-person exchange between associate and customer that they completely overlooked another way to deliver the experience.

What they failed to understand was that *the online experience was emerging as a new experience formerly delivered by frontline employees in an actual store.* Not moving quickly enough to reinvent the customer

experience into one that could be delivered online ultimately cost Blockbuster its life.

Think Online Before Frontline

With every passing year come new statistics about the mass migration to online shopping. The more people who shop online, the clearer it becomes that consumers' online shopping experience is as important as the in-store experience itself.

One could even argue that it's more important (well, at least *I'm* arguing that), and here's why. If you have a physical location for your customers to visit, it's likely they'll research your company, products, services, and even reputation online before they ever venture out of their house or business. Your web presence and its look, feel, usability, intuitiveness, and functionality – they all represent and may replace your physical space and the customer experience itself. There may be a live person in your physical store who greets your customers, guides them, or makes recommendations, but if your online presence can't do all of those things, you're probably not going to lead potential customers to your physical space or entice them to purchase online, let alone make them loyal.

The Blockbuster and Netflix story is *not* just about changing technology from VHS to DVD to Blu-Ray to streaming media. It's about the changing wants and needs of consumers who are focused on convenience and immediate gratification and satisfying those needs. For heaven's sake, toilet paper is now being ordered online and delivered to your house (at least mine is). Mr. Whipple of "Please don't squeeze the Charmin" fame isn't online telling you how soft the toilet paper is, but hundreds of customer reviews might be. Don't fool yourself – the ease of ordering commodities like toilet paper online is nice, but customers still want a great experience while they're doing it. They still want to be recognized, guided, advised, and appreciated, and it's your job to do that online.

Delivering a differentiated customer experience online – one that entices people to leave the house and visit your physical location or order through the internet – requires you to focus on components that may mirror an in-store experience but are, in fact, completely different.

- Your store planogram now becomes your online navigation.
- Displays are now photographs.
- Your store associate's recommendations and guidance are now transparent in customer reviews, comparison charts, and inventory.
- The cash wrap with a smiling associate who asks probing and open-ended questions is now your online check out.

If you're reading this book, you may already have an online presence and many if not all of those components above. I ask you to consider each of these components through a different lens:

- Think of each interaction as if your customer were in a physical location being assisted by a live person. What would that interaction look like? Feel like?
- Think of the online experience as just that. *It's not about transacting – it's about creating loyalty with your customers.*
- Do the people in your business who are responsible for the design, functionality, and programing of your online presence know your customer?
- Do they understand your products and services?
- Do they know the competitive landscape and your company's strategy to win in the marketplace?

These are must-haves — not nice-to-haves.

TRY THIS

- Identify each touchpoint of the online customer experience.
- Identify the employees or teams responsible for creating that online experience – programmers, web designers, etc.
- Teach individual online programmers and designers exactly who your customer is and what that customer expects at every touchpoint – not just the ones they're responsible for.
- To ensure a consistent customer experience, create in-person opportunities for your new "frontline" technology team to meet your actual customers and their counterparts on the *literal* frontline.

NOTES

NOTES

Chapter 5
The Ideal Customer Experience – The Final Frontier

Engaging your customer or potential customer in a differentiated experience is your only competitive advantage. We're in a global market where the same or similar products and services can be sourced from multiple places and where your competitors can knock off your "unique" offering overnight.

In this omni-channel world, the consumer or business customer has access to more information than ever, and they're making their decisions on what to buy and where to buy long before they walk into your store or call into your business. They're more knowledgeable than ever because of the unprecedented access to information. This can often reduce the actual number of touchpoints a customer has with a real live person in your business. Fewer touchpoints mean fewer opportunities to build loyalty person-to-person, so when you *do* have a live touchpoint, it has to be really meaningful. That touchpoint is a powerful determinant in whether someone buys that product from you or from your competitor. In most cases, price is not the determining factor in whether someone will buy and become loyal. *Emotion* is.

Your organization probably has a customer experience strategy. You've likely spent a lot of time and money identifying your core customer, their needs and wants, and your competition. Maybe you have some slick-looking PowerPoint decks about your strategy. You might have custom-built systems and processes to support and serve your identified customer. You may even think you're training your frontline to deliver the customer experience you envision.

This is all good, and your heart is in the right place. But just having a great product, environment, processes, systems, and trained employees is not enough. What else could I possibly ask of you? Consider this: *The customer experience never can and never will exceed your employees' experience.* Investing in your employees' experience and customer experience requires *the same level of commitment.*

What will make or break your success as an organization are your employees and your customer experience, *in that order.* This, my friends, is the final frontier.

My experience has shown me that many organizations rush to "train" employees to use the systems, processes, and technologies that support the customer experience strategy. In their hurry to train everybody, they miss several critical steps in actually *creating engaged employees* – those who are immersed in the experience themselves.

The customer experience never can and never will exceed your employees' experience.

Before training ever begins, employees need to know the big picture of the industry they serve, how your business fits into that story, and how each of them contributes to that story. They need to know they're part of your business's unique culture and brand and that they're empowered to bring that brand to life through every customer interaction. They must realize that they have the freedom and know-how to be authentically themselves in how they deliver the brand and yet remain consistent with the culture, values, and experience that marketing is promising and customers expect. Training on systems, processes, procedures, and technology is simply not enough. For your employees to create a differentiated experience, they must deliver a customer experience with their heads, hearts, and hands.

When you engage your employees as business partners, you help them see the business the same way your leaders see it. They are better equipped and more likely to bring their full contribution to the job and become loyal to the company. Loyal employees create loyal customers. That's not a new concept, but's hard to achieve – and well worth it.

Take a Walk in Your Customer's Sandals

Let's consider how two employees with very different *employee experiences* affect the customer experience.

These days, my wife and I are empty-nesters living in the heart of Chicago's Gold Coast that's filled with restaurants and shops from Michigan Avenue to Rush Street. A block from my house sits a clothing boutique bedecked with enticing and elaborate window displays of the latest fashions. It's part of a small local chain where the clothes are beautiful and pricey, for sure. My wife and I pass the store often, pressing our noses against the window to get a look at the trendy clothes and trendy people inside.

One day, my wife commented on a pair of sandals in the window of this boutique. "Those are gorgeous, but I'm sure they cost a fortune," she lamented. Another day, she said, "Look – those sandals are still there! I just *love* them." And later, "I wonder if they're as comfortable as they are sexy!" With each passing, my wife would deliver a new verbal love note to those sandals. She was *courting* them.

One Friday night, I came home from a weeklong business trip. How was I greeted? Not by "I missed you – welcome home!" but by "I finally broke down and bought those sandals I loved! Please don't ask how much they cost, because there is no justification." I looked down at her feet. She was wearing running shoes. She said, "Oh, they're still in the box. I'll wear them tomorrow." I said, "I'm glad you finally got them – I know how much you loved them. So how was the store?" She told me that the store was beautiful, but the help was kind of snooty – almost "too cool for school." But she'd seen some other things she'd liked, so she planned to return.

The next day, as part of our Saturday morning ritual, we set out for our local farmers' market. My wife proudly walked up to me wearing her beloved sandals and said, "What do you think?" Of course, I complimented her on her footwear as we stepped off the elevator into the lobby of our building and out the front door.

The *very second* my wife's foot hit the pavement, the seam at the front of her right sandal split open. She was horrified and said, "I can't believe this! I bought these at 5 o'clock last night! This is the first time I've had them on!" I told her not to worry, that the boutique was on the way to the market, and that we'd stop there first and exchange them.

Within minutes, we entered the boutique, which was filled with vibrant music, well-lit displays, and hip-looking sales associates. I made a beeline for the large round tufted banquette, the kind you see in sumptuous hotel lobbies, which was intended for waiting husbands. As I began a game of solitaire on my smartphone, I heard my wife talking to the salesperson and her flat reply, "I can't make an exchange on shoes without my manager's approval. Please wait."

My wife sat next to me for the next 20 minutes when she realized that the store manager had been on the phone behind the counter directly in front of us the entire time. There had been no acknowledgment of her presence, no mouthed "just a moment." Most of our good humor had been lost by the time my wife explained to the manager with the movie-star good looks how the seam had ripped within five minutes of wearing her sandal.

Both his tone and his reply were quick and definitive: "I'm sorry, but I can't help you. We don't take back shoes that have been worn."

To her credit, my wife did not explode. She presented the receipt for the shoes and spoke in short sentences. "I

bought these at 5 o'clock last night. It is now 10 am. I wore them from my home to the sidewalk. They broke immediately. That should not have happened. And I wore them *one block* to get here to exchange them."

The movie-star manager repeated, "I'm sorry, but I can't help you. We don't take back shoes that have been worn."

Standing on one leg, my wife held up the broken shoe to show that the product was defective, and the response was the same, with the addition of one word. He said, "*Regardless*, we don't take back shoes that have been worn."

At this point, I walked to the counter, picked up my 100-pound wife with one arm, took off her other shoe, placed both shoes on the counter, and said, "Well, you just did! You just took them back!" And I carried her out of the store.

Outside on the sidewalk, my barefoot wife called her credit card company to dispute the charge while I posted the story on Yelp. I found that my experience with this store had a lot of company – there were plenty of negative comments about this establishment.

Ninety minutes later, while we were shopping in another store just a few doors down, the district manager of that boutique chain called my wife's cell phone with an offer. "If you take down your Yelp comment," he said, "I'll refund your money." The audacity of this man to *negotiate* a refund was galling!

I was in such outrage that I yanked the phone from my wife's hand and said, "How about you refund my money because it's the right thing to do, and we'll never darken your doorstep again?"

He said, "Listen, the manager was just following the script. He should have taken the shoes back."

I said, "Well, he didn't, and the worst part was his inability to look at this particular scenario where the shoes were just purchased and worn for just moments. All he did was recite policy!"

The district manager said, "Yes, but again, he was simply following the script."

I let him know that scripts don't create loyal customers.

It didn't take us long to learn that literally every item and every brand we'd seen in that fancy boutique could be found in stores within 100 yards – including those sandals! We soon entered another retailer with similar products but a very different personality.

In this second store, a saleswoman immediately approached my wife and said, "Oh, you're a petite! I'm a petite too, and I specialize in dressing petite women. We're going to have fun today!" She quickly put my wife in a dressing room and began bringing her things to look at while she asked questions about her likes and dislikes. She really took the time to get to know her. And we walked out of that store with several bags of clothes – and those same beautiful sandals.

So within a few hours, one business not only lost a sale for that day but a customer for life – one who lives in the neighborhood, loves fashion, and takes pride in her wardrobe – and another gained a customer who is now loyal, demonstrated through relationships and repeat purchases. And the funny thing is, my wife has to walk three blocks farther to buy the same clothes but have a totally different experience – and she does it gladly.

That business not only lost a sale for that day, but a customer for life.

From the Employees' Point of View

So we know what that story looks like through the eyes of the customer. But what's the difference in the employees' experience in both of these scenarios?

The Manager in Store 1:
- Was nice and approachable.
- Made a great professional impression, suited to a well-known high-end shop.
- Was engaged in rules and regulations, immersed in processes and procedures, and likely held accountable to deliver on them.

- Focused on upholding store policy unquestionably (as he was probably rewarded on enforcing it).

This manager was simply unable to see the whole picture. His response to a problem was to read the script that his corporate office had trained him on regarding a policy. He showed no signs of being rooted in a customer culture and no empowerment to bring his brand to life in this guest's experience. In fact, it felt as if the entire staff was doing customers a favor by allowing them to enter the store! (Maybe that *was* the culture. Interesting.)

So instead of doing the right thing for this particular customer, creating an experience that was memorable, turning a negative into a positive, and having that customer possibly spend more money, that manager ended up in this book as a bad example.

The Salesperson in Store 2:
- Was nice and approachable.
- Made a great professional impression, suited to a well-known high-end shop.
- Was engaged in the customer experience, not just company policy.
- Focused on what her store could offer the customer and her own great experience in working there.

The salesperson in the second store actually professed her love for the company, telling us how many years she had worked for the company and the different store locations she had worked in over the years. She told us how she was rewarded for her work by being sent to New York annually to meet with fashion designers who asked for her input on the kind of clothes she would sell and why. She was proud that she'd been Salesperson of the Year for that store several years in a row. It was clear that she understood the big picture, was rooted in a customer culture, and felt empowered to bring her organization's brand to life in every guest experience.

She was having a great employee experience and, consequently, was able to deliver a great customer experience. In fact, she and my wife now text about clothes and have become friends!

Now, not every retail experience needs to culminate in friendship, but in a world where the same brands are available right next door, customer experience is the true differentiator.

TRY THIS

- Hire people who love people. You can always train them on product.
- Engage your employees in delivering the *spirit* of the policies you establish, not just reciting the fine print.
- Empower your employees to make decisions that support the desired customer experience.
- Rebrand your customer service associates to "customer fanatics" and define what that means for your company.

NOTES

NOTES

Chapter 6
The Customer Journey

Creating loyal customers – isn't that what most companies are trying to do? It's pretty clear that's the endgame, but with today's competitive marketplace, it can get hazy in a hurry.

These days, organizations are spending a lot of time and money learning about their "customer's journey" – what customers are experiencing on the road to becoming loyal or dissatisfied with their company, in all its phases. Of course, knowing your customer's journey is very important because it allows you and your employees to understand and focus on the various touchpoints your customers experience on their way to making a purchase, while showing employees their direct impact on the customer experience.

The customer's journey has three phases: Before, During, and After. It doesn't get simpler than that!

There are mapping companies who offer "unique, proprietary, revolutionary" ways of creating complicated graphs and charts illustrating every minute detail of your customer's journey. (That's not necessarily a criticism or an approval, just an observation, but just looking at one of these can make your head spin.)

The goal is basic: to understand what your customer is going through and design the best possible journey for them. I'd like to suggest a simpler way to map your customer journey: *Before, During, and After.* It doesn't get simpler than that! Each phase is an opportunity to build customer loyalty.

Let's explore each component more deeply.

Before

Awareness – Before a purchase ever happens, the customer must become aware that they have a need or a desire that they need to or want to fulfill.

We'll follow a customer, Arden, who just moved from a condominium to a house. As Arden proudly pulls into the driveway after closing, he thinks, "Hey, I'm going to need a lawnmower – I've never had grass before!" He is now *aware* that he has a *need*. As his kids pile out of the back seat, they spot a cool trampoline in a nearby yard. They now have a *desire* to have a trampoline in their own backyard.

Interest – The customer wants to learn more about options for products or services, and investigates.

Arden's new neighbors stop by to greet him. He's *interested* in the kind of lawnmowers they use and asks questions about the features they prefer. He also asks how their kids like the trampoline. Later, he goes online to research lawnmowers and trampolines.

Consideration – The customer actively works to clearly define his or her needs and desires, deciding to satisfy them or do nothing.

Arden is deluged by more options than he can process! He realizes he must further define his specific needs and determine his satisfaction criteria for both products. He *considers* the size of his yard and whether he needs a riding or standing mower, an electric or gas mower, one that self-mulches or uses a bag, and all the other options. Arden then looks at trampolines — different styles and sizes — and he wonders which ones offer the best safety features for his kids.

During
Purchase – The customer engages with the actual product or service, the company selling it, and its people (in-store or online), and makes a purchase.

Arden determines the right mower that will meet his needs. He finds enough information on the company's website to feel confident *buying* it online, and does so.

He's still unsure about the safety issues of the trampoline, so he takes the next step by visiting a sporting goods store and *looking* at the actual trampoline. Arden finds a well-displayed, well-inventoried store with friendly sales associates. He asks to speak with someone familiar with the trampoline he wants to buy. He's introduced to a *"nexpert"* (Remember from Chapter 4?) who is knowledgeable as well as authentic in his recommendations – in fact, he owns one himself. With his concerns addressed and feeling confident, Arden purchases the trampoline.

First Use – The customer uses the product or service without aid for the first time, beginning to measure it against expectations.

It's a busy Saturday for Arden! As soon as he returns from the sporting goods store with the trampoline, the kids are begging him to set it up, but he has to take care of the lawn first, with his new mower that's still in the shipping box. Arden examines it, figures out how it works, learns about the gears and functions, and then *uses it for the first time* – while his kids fidget in the driveway begging him to hurry. With the lawn finished, Arden sets up the trampoline, safety net and all. The very second the last screw is in place, the kids are jumping and laughing to their hearts' delight.

Ongoing Use – The customer uses the product or service regularly, discovering new needs and/or problems.

After a couple of months at the new house, Arden realizes that he needs to rake dead grass each time he mows the lawn. The self-mulching feature *isn't working up to his expectations.* On the other hand, his kids and their new friends can be found jumping on the trampoline every day after school, and even having sleepovers on it on the weekends. It's *safe, durable, and a source of joy* and exercise for the whole family.

After

Additional Purchase – The customer looks back on the overall experience with the product or service, deciding to buy more of the product or service or other adjacent products or services.

As Arden thinks about his lawnmower purchase, he's happy with the customer experience as far as the ability to buy it online and the prompt delivery, but he's unhappy with the product itself. *He is dissatisfied.* He also needs a weedwhacker and hedge trimmer to maintain his property, and he starts the buying process again with this new awareness. It wasn't that he had a bad experience per se, but he's dissatisfied enough to investigate, consider, and purchase from another company.

As for the trampoline, Arden was delighted with the expertise he received at the sporting goods store and equally delighted with the product. *He was satisfied.* Later that summer, when his kids ask for a volleyball net and ball, he remembers his experience with the sporting goods store, the "nexpert," and even the manufacturer of the trampoline. He returns to that store and buys the equipment from them.

Referral – The customer shares positive or negative recommendations directly or indirectly with other people.

Arden hosts an end-of-summer barbecue for his neighbors. He entertains them with stories of moving to a new neighborhood and the work he's done on the house. His neighbors talk about how his backyard has become the gathering place for all the kids in the neighborhood. Arden *shares his great experiences* with the "nexpert" at the sporting goods store and in an online review on the company's website. When another neighbor jokes about how Arden spends his Saturdays raking dead grass, Arden doesn't hesitate to *tell his guests how dissatisfied* he is with the lawnmower and the company he purchased it from.

So that's the customer journey from Arden's perspective. Now, let's see what it looks like from a business perspective.

Before

Before any customer investigates your product or service, your *company must be clear* on what you're bringing to the marketplace. With the understanding of your customer's focus, you can then set about *getting into the minds of your customer* to identify their specific needs and desires, *ensure that you meet their needs,* and start *promoting* your products and services, based on your brand promise.

Before

☐ Be clear on your products and/or services

☐ Get into your customers' minds

☐ Be sure your products and/or services meet their needs

☐ Promote your products and/or services

During

With your products and service offerings in place, companies and customers *connect* through the web, mobile apps, call centers, and physical locations. As we learned in the previous chapter, whatever the mode that the customer chooses to interact with you, companies need to create a meaningful touchpoint or deliver a great customer experience. (And as we learned with Arden, in both of his purchases – online and in-person – he had great customer experiences. And in the case of the trampoline, his online experience led him to a physical location.)

Once your customer is at your front door – telephonically, electronically, or physically – it's time to *engage them*. (My close friend Phil reminds me on a regular basis that you only get one chance to make a first impression, and in this competitive marketplace, yours has got to be great.) Your company must decide how it will deliver a *level of service* that <u>customers</u> *determine is important to them in the decision-making process*. This can run the gamut from a user-friendly website with no human contact all the way to a high-touch in-person interaction, as long as you engage them in a way that gives them a great customer experience.

During

- ☐ Connect with your customers
- ☐ Engage your customers
- ☐ Provide a level of service that customers desire
- ☐ Help them make a decision

After

With the decision made and the product in the hands of your customer, you want to make sure your customers return – in fact, you want them to become *loyal*. There is an opportunity at *checkout* to provide a smooth last step while inviting customers to *continue their relationship with you*. Once they leave your website, mobile app, call center, or store, there is an opportunity to *ask for feedback, extend incentives, and send positive reminders* about your company.

After

☐ Make checkout smooth and easy

☐ Invite customers to continue the relationship

☐ Ask for feedback

☐ Extend incentives and send positive reminders

When engaging your employees in the customer's journey, remember to keep it simple. Help them recognize that the customer's journey is matched at each step with the journey of your business. When – and only when – these journeys are in lockstep can you create and execute an experience that drives loyalty.

TRY THIS

- Simplify your customer's journey into just three phases – Before, During, and After.
- Determine your desired outcomes at the end of each phase.
- Evaluate current touchpoints to uncover gaps between the current outcomes and your desired ones.
- Rework touchpoints as necessary so you can deliver those desired outcomes.

NOTES

NOTES

Chapter 7
Start with a Customer First Culture, and Start at the Top

We all agree that businesses looking to succeed aim to provide the ultimate customer experience. And as we discussed in Chapter 4, the customer experience your business offers *can never and will never exceed your employees' experience.* In fact, your customer culture is a direct reflection of your employee culture. And who's responsible for creating a superior employee experience? Your HR department? Your "people" people? Nope. It's the CEO. And here's why.

Your customer experience can never and will never exceed your employees' experience.

The employee experience is a critical part of how a CEO's success is measured – maybe not by CEOs themselves or their boards, but certainly by their employees and even customers. After all, if the people responsible for engaging customers aren't *having* a great experience, how can they be expected to *deliver* a great experience?

You've likely heard of the "service-profit chain." It's been around for decades, and it's still valid and meaningful today. It's a point of view that illustrates why your customer experience can't possibly surpass your employees' experience.

The service-profit chain shows how customer loyalty and employee satisfaction are linked:

| Effective
Leadership | Team
Member
Engagement | Customer
Engagement
Satisfaction | Revenue,
Loyalty, and
Profitability |

- Profit and growth result from customer loyalty.
- Loyalty comes from customer satisfaction.
- Customer satisfaction is determined by the value of services provided.
- Value flows from loyal, productive employees.
- Employee satisfaction is a result of a customer first culture, leadership, and the support needed to be successful, allowing employees to deliver satisfaction to customers…who become loyal.

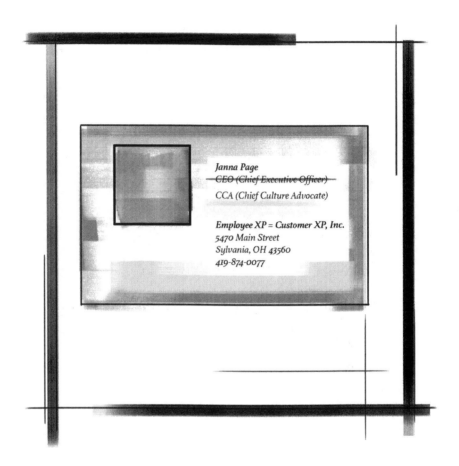

Janna Page
~~CEO (Chief Executive Officer)~~
CCA (Chief Culture Advocate)

Employee XP = Customer XP, Inc.
5470 Main Street
Sylvania, OH 43560
419-874-0077

In striving to deliver a great customer experience, there are three steps, which we'll look at one by one in this section of the book:

1. Creating a customer first culture
2. Empowering managers to act like owners
3. Delivering an authentic experience at the front line

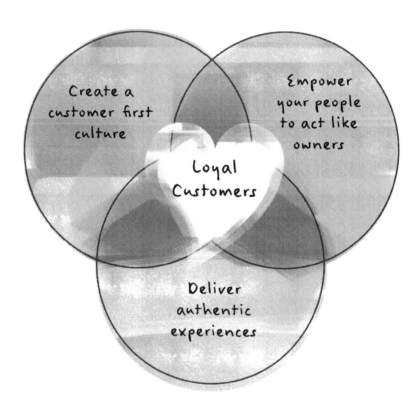

It All Begins with Culture

Notice that "culture" is number one. Let's start with a definition: Organizational culture is the *shared values and beliefs* that govern the way people in that organization behave. These shared values influence the way people act and perform, and they shape the decisions people make at work. A strong culture – good or bad – is something you can actually feel when you walk in the door, whether you're an employee or a customer. Customer first culture means the customer has a seat at the strategy table. We have to design all of our touchpoints, processes, hiring practices, and technology with the needs and desires of our customers first.

Everything rests on the shoulders of your culture. You can have the greatest customer experience strategy in the world, but culture eats strategy for breakfast every day. Yet, more often than not, I see leaders focused on creating strategy while delegating culture and the customer experience to someone outside of the C-Suite.

And yes, your organization *has* a culture. Whether it's been well crafted or it's simply evolved over time, you do have one. But is it the culture that you need, that your employees need, that will support the customer experience that you want to deliver? Do the leaders of your business really understand the culture at the store level? When was the last time your leaders actually worked a shift or served a customer? Spending even one shift with a frontline employee can be eye-opening and can help a leader understand the realities of the customer experience as well as the employee experience. In this dynamic lies the popularity of the TV show *Undercover Boss*, where incognito CEOs learn what's really going on. If you can get your leaders to the front lines, they'll learn a lot – disguise optional.

Your culture – and thus, your employees' experience – must be led by the CEO and the leadership team. If the top leaders in your company don't own the culture, can't accurately define the culture, don't know whether it's a customer first culture, or aren't sure if it's delivering a great employee/customer experience, red flags should be flying!

Here's what I mean. I worked with a money-lending retail store where there were co-CEOs. One was focused on operations, and the other on the customer experience. The second one started each day by reading every single customer comment, good or bad, from social media, email, and snail mail.

Similarly, PIRCH San Diego, an up-and-coming multi-unit chain that's redefining how people buy appliances, has become instantly famous for the culture they've created. Their CEO responds to every customer complaint. He even publishes his own phone number and email address so customers can reach him directly.

To find out where your leadership stands, email or individually present these questions to the leaders in your business, and ask them to be honest.

- How would you describe our company's culture today?
- What metrics are you using to measure its success?
- Who is responsible for crafting, delivering, and sustaining our culture?
- What is your role, specifically, as it relates to our culture?
- What is the impact of our culture on our business performance today?

Look at the answers from all of your leaders. If your leadership team is not aligned on the meaning and state of your culture and on their own roles in sustaining it, how can your *employees* be clear on what it means? How can *they* deliver the desired customer experience?

And that's why it's baffling that culture is so often delegated by the very leaders who must be the *owners* of culture!

No Hand-Offs, Please

My experience tells me that CEOs readily agree that a customer first culture is important – in fact, it's critical to the success of their brand. And just as quickly as they agree that it's critical, they delegate it to somebody else. "Here, go do that culture thing, and you have my full support" can be heard echoing down the hallways.

Attention CEOs! This question is specifically for you:
If you want a customer first culture, you have to live it for yourself, model the behaviors, reward and recognize those

who are bringing it to life, and enforce accountability or consequences for those who opt out.   So if culture is key to the success of your strategy and customer experience, and these are key measures on your scorecard as a CEO, how can you possibly delegate it?

The answer is this: *You can't delegate a customer first culture!* It must be designed, embodied, and demonstrated at the highest level of the business, starting with the CEO. A customer first culture means the customer and the employee have seats at the table when every business decision is made by the top executives – if not literally, at least figuratively.

I recently gave a speech on customer experience, and during Q&A, an HR professional told me that her CEO had assigned her the job of creating a customer-centric culture. She explained she was at first flattered, honored, and excited about the assignment. But by her fourth month on the job, she still hadn't been able to get space on the CEO's calendar to discuss it. She knew she couldn't create culture in a vacuum or without the participation and buy-in of the leaders. She was concerned – and rightfully so – for the success of the organization, the culture, and her job. She saw no way she could be successful. She told me, "If the leaders don't think the culture is important and aren't part of its creation, it will never be successful – and neither will I."

This is an all-too-common story. Creating a culture that ultimately leads to an excellent customer experience isn't a tactic or a technical issue to be dealt with. You can't just treat it as a leaking pipe, where you make a call and someone comes to fix it while you're off doing something else.

So How Do You Create This Culture?

The new brand of progressive business minds understands the value chain. Companies like Parker, Virgin America, Uber, and Netflix know their markets and prospective buyers. They make sure their employees can convey this culture to buyers and adjust it to their markets. They can't be drones – they know how to be themselves while offering a consistent customer experience to every customer, every time. Their managers are empowered to make decisions that support the success of the business, the needs of the customers, and the engagement of the employees. And all this happens consistently, whether the shopping experience is online, in a small-town store, or in a busy downtown kiosk.

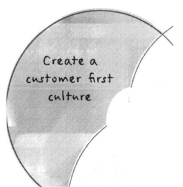

Create a customer first culture

You can talk about customer experience all day long, but until you start to *live* it as a culture, it's just lip service. Putting the customer at the center of your business is key, and here's how you can make it happen:

1. Clarify and align on your culture.

The CEO and top leaders must agree on a definition of the culture needed to create loyalty and distinguish your business from the competition. Without a clear picture that everyone understands in the same way, using the same words, you run the risk of failure right from the start. Culture just can't be created based on personal opinion. You need to know the facts. There should be no room for personal interpretation.

Go beyond the *words* you use for your culture definition. Many teams believe that when they say the same words, they're aligned on the meaning behind them. That's not always the case. When my boys were teenagers and I'd say, "I want to see your rooms *clean*," their definitions for the word "clean" were certainly not the same as mine. And so it goes with culture – you often say the same words and mean different things. Be very sure that the customer experience you're defining means the same thing to every member of the leadership team.

And the most important thing: When you define your culture, be *especially* sure that the definition is informed by what your *customer* actually wants that experience to be. Instead of inventing a customer experience on their own, leaders should gather insights directly from customers and define the culture based on what's most important to them. First, understand the customers' definition of the experience they want, and then work to bring that to life.

Another good tactic is to find positive things that are already occurring naturally – what's going on in the store that's outperforming all the others in its region, or the hotel where customer satisfaction scores are highest. Learn what's unique about how they're delivering the customer experience. Then prototype it and replicate it across the business. Often, businesses – especially those with distributed business models – have unique cultures within different departments or different store locations. Your job is to find the cultural bright spots and replicate them.

2. Deploy your culture.

Once leaders understand the *current* culture and the *desired* culture, it's time to engage all employees in executing that new culture. In order for everyone in your organization to adopt a new culture – to focus on the customer first – they must have a clear understanding of what the culture is today, see the same clear picture of what the customer first culture will look like tomorrow, and envision a well-defined path that will bridge the gap.

This is complex stuff! Your job is to make it simple so everyone can understand it. Make it personal, relevant, and fun. A PowerPoint deck and an emailed memo from the CEO definitely won't pull on the heartstrings of your people.

> Not long ago, I sat with a CEO who shared his disappointment about a recent email he'd sent to all his employees internationally. The subject line of the

email read, "Urgent Message from the CEO." The message presented a high-level overview of the business priorities for the next fiscal year, with specific actions he was asking employees to take.

As the week went by, he was surprised and disappointed that he didn't receive more comments and reactions about the email. And as more time passed, he was even more surprised that he wasn't seeing any change happening, as he had requested. He wondered if some technical error had occurred, so he asked his IT department to check – had the email really been sent to everyone on the list? They came back with upsetting news: 78% of the recipients hadn't even *opened* the email that spelled out the strategic priorities from the CEO. He was shocked. I wasn't!

Changing your culture is a bold move. You need to take bold steps to engage your employees. You can't do it with an email.

As the leader of the customer experience culture, it's the job of the CEO to literally paint the picture of what that culture looks like using storytelling and visual imagery. *Emotion* must be attached to the words. If you want your employees to create an emotional connection between your *culture and customers*, start by creating an emotional connection between your *employees and your culture*.

Culture is three-dimensional. Culture is meant to be immersive. It's meant to be experienced, to be felt. It's the soul of your business. Your business already has a customer experience culture. Is it the one you want?

The CEO and the leadership team must be ready and willing to demonstrate the new culture.

3. Sustain your culture.
This goes beyond financial commitment. A large part is *living* the changes. The CEO and the leadership team must be ready and willing to demonstrate that new culture. Leaders go first – that's why they're called *leaders*. This means taking risks in the name of your culture, your employees, your customers, and your future.

Many leaders make the same error when introducing a new culture – they "announce" it at a town hall meeting and expect it to instantly become part of everyday life. *That won't work.* To sustain a new customer first culture – or any kind, for that matter – it has to be constantly talked about, articulated, and explained at every possible opportunity. Give examples, present ideas for improvement, highlight individual or team successes every time you have an audience, large or small. Get excited about it so your employees can get excited about it. CEOs and other leaders need to breathe life into the culture by talking about it at every interaction – verbal, written, or unspoken.

Sustaining the culture also means funding the change with investments that may include advancing the skills and capabilities of your leadership team, your managers, and front-line employees. CEOs and leaders also may have to change the way they support, appraise, and reward skills and behaviors. The same old standards may not apply in the new culture. You'll need to determine what winning looks like, what success looks like in this new environment, and find ways of supporting, enhancing, and rewarding those skills and behaviors. This may require an overhaul in your compensation, commission, and bonus structure. After all, culture is essentially determined by the actions and behaviors we reward and those we simply won't tolerate. Your compensation structure must align with the actions and behaviors that drive the culture you want.

Many companies claim to have a customer first culture. But unless the culture is well defined, it's doomed to fail. And if it's not a top priority for the CEO, it's not likely to ever be for the people who are engaging customers in stores, call centers, or online. Creating a winning customer first culture is about commitment, from the leaders to the customers. You can't just delegate it and throw money at it; you actually have to live it – not through proclamations, speeches, and announcements, but by actions and behaviors. If leaders don't see this as part of their job, a successful customer experience won't be a part of the future of the business…it's that important.

Putting Culture to Work at Costco, from the Top Down

In the sometimes-impersonal world of big-box stores, Costco stands out as a shining example of delivering a great customer experience, and Costco's customer loyalty is the industry's highest. Not only that, but its employees love working at Costco. Their employees are the highest paid in the big-box segment, and all stakeholders are pleased with their profitability.

I wanted to know why, so I went to Costco to find out more. Costco is not my client, and I've never done work for them or visited their corporate offices. I'm just a member. But even as "just a member," I was able to get a direct quote from the CEO by simply picking up the phone and calling. I got responses to questions about Costco's culture from employees with just one email. The responses were friendly and engaging, and people were quick to offer permission to use them. I've never had such a pleasant experience dealing with a corporate staff. This tells me volumes about the way they truly live a culture focused on the customer.

This is an organization that understands how and why focusing on employees first leads to the loyalty and service that customers expect.

Here's what CEO Jim Sinegal told me:

"Costco takes prides in its Members First culture that's embedded in its return policy. We have among the most lenient return policies in retail. Why? Because it's one of the most dreaded aspects of the retail experience for customers. We don't force our members to jump through hoops to get a refund, even if the product was abused, mishandled, or used and returned after a typical life expectancy. Only a small percentage of members abuse the policy, and it engenders loyalty in everybody else. Our return policy implicitly says to members that we trust them."

So policies are just that – policies. But how did the managers and employees at Costco come to understand the *culture* behind the policy? When I asked their employees that question, they told me this:

"Jim sets the tone when he answers his own phone."
"Jim never considered having a PR Department."
"Jim's direction was always simple and straightforward: Do the right thing. Tell the truth. And when you make a mistake, fix the problem."

The actions and behaviors demonstrated by this CEO helped to set the tone for his employees and this customer first culture.

TRY THIS

- Help your leaders understand why they must lead an employee/customer first culture if they want to achieve the company's goals.
- Create an ROI case that demonstrates how culture impacts the customer experience, and how the customer experience impacts loyalty and profitability.
- Identify actions and behaviors that should be rewarded and those that shouldn't be tolerated in a customer first culture.
- Encourage leaders to develop a compensation structure that supports the actions and behaviors that will create a customer first culture.
- Urge leaders to get out of the office – to live the culture and demonstrate it to employees at every level. Employees will follow the actions and behaviors of leaders before they will ever adopt a culture expressed in an email, through a PowerPoint presentation, or on a poster in the back room.
- Get your leaders to the front line – they can forget what it's like to be there.
- List things you'd change about the culture to improve the employee experience and ultimately the customer experience.

NOTES

NOTES

Chapter 8
Today's Managers…
Yesterday's Shopkeepers

Customers can feel the culture, tone, and atmosphere of a store the moment they enter. Who determines that culture? Is it determined by the corporate office where all of the planning, branding, marketing, and advertising is done? Is it determined by the frontline employees who spend most of their day preparing the store for customers and working with them? No. These are factors, but the key determinant of the culture of any store is the manager.

Just like yesterday's shopkeepers — their predecessors — a store manager's personality, leadership style, and ability to engage employees and customers alike determine the culture and even the success or failure of any business location. Managers are the linchpin to a successful business. Investing in their development is not only important in retaining them and critical to reducing employee turnover but — believe it or not — it's also an essential part of delivering a differentiated customer experience.

You've likely heard the saying, "Employees don't quit companies — they quit managers." I'd ask you to consider the following: "Customers don't quit your businesses — they quit your employees." There is a direct and important connection between how a manager engages an employee and how that employee engages the customer. Making sure that your managers are equipped to be successful should be at the top of your list of things to consider when you're focusing on your customers' experience.

Empower your people to act like owners

What Makes a Manager Successful?

All great managers have one thing in common that helps them create successful results for their business, employees, and customers: They act like owners. And they do it in four specific ways:

1. They know their business: the marketplace, the competition, and the consumers.
2. They see their role as "Chief Engagement Officer," not as a superhero individual contributor wearing a manager's badge.
3. They engage their teams in the culture, business, strategy, and in delivering the customer experience.
4. They drive results through their employees.

These are exactly the same things that their predecessors understood. The shopkeepers who excelled at these four skills were successful, and those who didn't were forced to shutter their stores.

So how do great managers acquire these skills? Are they born that way, like natural entrepreneurs, or can these skills be learned? For some managers, these things *do* come naturally. But most managers have been promoted to that level because they were fantastic individual contributor employees with no natural ability to be a great manager. And they need help.

My experience tells me two important things. First, managers who have these skills run businesses that are successful. Second, managers are the most underinvested employee segment in business today. Investments in leadership development are immense, and even more is invested in frontline training. But managers are left to figure out how to do their job on their own.

To illustrate the difference between managers who act like owners and those who are simply promoted to manager because they were terrific employees, let me present two personal experiences. It's likely that you've have had similar incidents yourself.

> Managers are the most underinvested employee segment in business. They're left to figure out how to do their job on their own.

"Hey, I'm Right Here!"

My wife and I were shopping for a piece of artwork for our new condo in Chicago. We stopped at an upscale store that's famous for its avant-garde decor. I spotted a 4x4-foot photo framed in Plexiglas – Hugh Hefner smoking a pipe in the basement of the original Playboy mansion on State Street in Chicago, surrounded by

Playboy bunnies, circa 1968. Now, what says "Chicago" more than that? I had to have it! My wife objected to the rather high price, so I decided to see if it came in a smaller size or if they had something similar, priced a bit more moderately. I said to the salesperson, "I love this picture, but does it come in another size? I wasn't looking to spend this much money." She said, "It's one-of-a-kind and it doesn't come in any other size." And she walked away!

However, the store manager was standing nearby, and he'd heard the conversation. He said, "Sir, have you purchased with us before?" I said, "No, I haven't, but I've been window shopping with you for months." "Oh great," he said. "I can give you a first-time-customer 10% discount on that piece."

Needless to say, I bought it – and then went on to spend *more* money in that store on this same shopping trip. Given that this store had merchandise that I liked, was in my neighborhood, and had a manager who was able to make decisions in the moment to create a great customer experience, I had taken my first step to becoming a loyal customer.

As ridiculous as it sounds, I carried that very heavy 4x4-foot Plexiglas-and-steel picture on my head ten blocks to my condo and, that very same day, returned to that store to do some more shopping. The manager wasn't there this time, nor was the first sales associate we encountered. We met someone completely new. When I asked for his help choosing bath mats, he said, "All of our bathmats are custom-made. Why don't you look online and order from there?"

Hmmm. I'm standing *right here in the store.* You have floor samples of bath mats *right in front of me.* You have a chance to help me with a custom product and take my order now. Why would you send me out of the store with the very real chance I may never order it online (which I didn't because the process was too complicated, and I just gave up).

The manager had opened the door to a long-term, loyal customer relationship – not because he offered a discount, but because he acted like a shopkeeper/owner when it came to servicing me as a customer. However, two front-line employees quickly eroded that loyalty: the sales clerk who curtly told me the picture didn't come in another size and walked away, and the employee who dismissed me to go online instead of helping me in the store.

So…is the manager the hero? Not unless he waits on every customer! This is an example of a great individual contributor wearing a manager's badge. He was, in fact, what I would call a *bad* manager. He was actually a very competent salesperson who could act as a 1960s shop owner when it came to pleasing a customer and negotiating a price, but he lacked the ability to engage his employees in delivering the customer experience in the same way he did. He was paying attention to the customers in the store, listening to wants and needs, and coming up with solutions, but his employees weren't. Managers can't wait on every customer, and it's not their job to do so.

Bottom line: While this manager did a great job of acting like an owner in how he negotiated the sale with me, he missed several critical elements of being a great manager. He didn't understand that his role was to engage his team and drive results through them. And the result was the loss of a potential loyal customer.

Now, compare that story to this one, which has a very different ending.

"Help Me Help My Customer"

One beautiful day, I was waiting to go to an afternoon movie. I also needed a new navy blue sport coat and some dress shirts. With 15 to 20 minutes to kill, I stepped into a mid-level men's clothing store, part of a national chain. An associate greeted me immediately and asked how she could help. Smiling, she mentioned that she was new, and that she might need assistance from her manager in outfitting me. Within a moment, the manager was by her side to coach her.

The associate asked me what I was looking for, and the manager chimed in to determine the size, color, and fit that I wanted. I made them both laugh by saying that all I really wanted was something to hide my love handles. Then, the manager turned to the associate and said, "Why don't we show him XYZ?" He led both of us to the appropriate rack and explained the design and cut to both of us, pointing out how it would meet my needs. In essence, he was educating her and selling to me at the same time.

I didn't have time on that visit to shop for shirts, but I returned on another day. By then, this sales associate had gained more experience. As she greeted me, it was clear that she remembered who I was. I asked her how she was doing, and she told me that she was working more hours and really enjoying her work.

By herself, she led me directly to the shirts I was looking for and pointed out the size and style I wanted. I could tell she had been developed to understand the products they carried and how to match them to customers' needs. In a few short weeks, she had gone from an uncertain novice to an advisor.

While I was trying on some shirts, the manager saw me and came over to say hello. He asked if I was getting everything I needed, and he assured me that I was in good hands, which I was. This manager, while acknowledging me, didn't have to be involved in the details of the sale. He could focus on the overall store – all the customers and all the employees – because he understood the marketplace he was serving, knew his role as Chief Engagement Officer, had obviously engaged his team, and realized how to drive results through them. In this case, all his efforts led to investing in developing an employee who could deliver the type of experience he wanted in his store for his customers.

I'm not sure if it was because my professional focus is on customer experience or because the associate was about the same age as my sons, but I was truly *in the process* – I wanted her to be successful! I witnessed an employee start to grow in her ability to deliver the customer experience. I felt like we were in the game together. Not only did I want to go back to this store to shop, I wanted to go back to visit *them*. I have an emotional connection. I'm a loyal customer. And it's because this manager acted like an owner.

Those Four Skills Endure

In the first story, the manager failed to engage his employees in delivering the desired customer experience. That manager stepped in to take over and saved one sale but lost another. In the second story, I got a great customer experience from a new employee who didn't know a French cuff from a coat hanger — but who had a manager that understood his role in helping her act like an owner. And that's what made my store visit personal, simple, and truly a pleasure — *and* won a loyal customer.

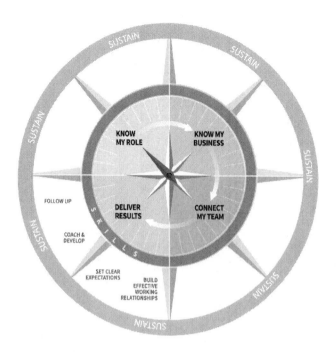

So, those four managers' skills endure over time – since the 1960s shopkeepers and before. Today's companies must help every one of their managers to master these things:

- Knowing their business: the marketplace, the competition, and the consumers.
- Seeing their role as "Chief Engagement Officer," not as a superhero individual contributor wearing a manager's badge.
- Engaging their teams in the business, the strategy, and in delivering the customer experience.
- Driving results through their employees.

This isn't easy, but empowering managers to act like owners is an investment in delivering a world-class customer experience.

TRY THIS

- Invest in your managers – take them offline to learn about your business and their role in it.
- Immerse managers in an understanding of your industry, the marketplace you serve, and your strategy to win.
- Allow your managers to make decisions as if they were the owners of their store, while upholding the standards of the business.
- Build your managers' skills so they can be CEOs – Chief Engagement Officers – of their teams.

NOTES

NOTES

Chapter 9
"I Gotta Be Me"

The people who serve your customers represent your business with every action and every interaction. Every time they do, they're either building or eroding your brand in the eyes of the consumer. With this in mind, organizations do their best to prepare frontline employees for success. Training, scripts, coaching, and the dreaded employee manual are just some of the ways that organizations guide the customer experience so that frontline employee/customer interactions are consistent and support the brand.

Employees can't build rapport or show enthusiasm when they're speaking from a script.

But all of that, while developed with the best of intentions, is about the company and may be even about the customer, but rarely takes into account the frontline people who are actually *delivering* that experience! What about *them?* What about what *they* bring to the table – their natural strengths, personalities, and experiences? What if companies allowed employees to be truly authentic in the way they interact with customers? I've found this authenticity to be the most important ingredient in the "secret sauce" of delivering a great customer experience from the front line.

The human touchpoint is the biggest variable in customer loyalty – and also the biggest determinant of that loyalty. Employees need freedom to be their authentic selves, and it's what customers will best relate to. Customers know when they're having an authentic experience. They gravitate to such an experience because that's the foundation of a real relationship, and relationships are the key to building customer loyalty.

But most companies focus solely on the customer. They strive to understand what the customer needs and wants to experience, and then attempt to script their employees to deliver it. *This alone won't work!* You must invest in helping your frontline employees to create interactions that are genuine and real. Employees can't build rapport or show passion and enthusiasm when they're speaking from a script. The customer experience happens in real time and is real life. You can't script real life!

Doing It All

To succeed in delivering great customer experiences, companies need to allow employees to add their own ingredient to that "secret sauce," to make that human connection with the customer. The key is to allow them to be their authentic selves *and at the same time* uphold the guidelines and brand of the company.

Imagine you were asked to be on stage all day, every day, and to follow a script the entire time, all in the name of representing a brand or product or service? Is that sustainable? Even if it were, would you *enjoy* doing

that? Would you be engaged? No! Clearly, we can't be something we're not eight hours a day, five days a week.

Deliver authentic experiences

So here's the challenge – we have to enable our frontline employees to:

- Deliver a consistent customer experience
- Uphold our brand standards and promises
- Do that while being truly themselves

This can be done, and is being done very successfully in some places. Check these examples.

Two Ways to Serve a Cold, Wet, Tired Traveler

I travel for business four days a week, 48 weeks a year, so I spend a lot of nights in hotels. On this particular trip, I landed in a city in a southern state at 11:30 on a hot summer night. My flight had been delayed due to a nasty storm, and it was still raining when I arrived. To make matters even more unpleasant, when I was leaving the rental car lot, I accidentally backed over one of those "Don't Back Over This" bumps. I had destroyed the tires and ripped out the entire bottom of the car. I spent the next hour filling out insurance paperwork, getting a new rental car, and finding the correct way to exit the lot.

When I arrived at the hotel at nearly 1:00 am, I was sopping wet, miserable, exhausted, and totally stressed out. As I entered the lobby, I was greeted by a woman with pink hair, a pierced eyebrow, and several colorful tattoos, dressed in the company uniform. She smiled at me, and said, "Hey, Gary! You finally got here!"

Those were the most beautiful words I'd heard all day. When I asked her how she knew who I was, she said I was the only man who hadn't checked in for the night. She called up my file on the computer and exclaimed, "Duuude! You have a shitload of points! You need to take a vacation and use 'em." I agreed.

She continued, "Hey, you look totally wiped. I know you've stayed with us before, so do you really want me to explain our amenities, or would you like to get to your room right away?" I nodded at the last choice, and she quickly and efficiently sent me on my way.

That particular check-in was much more memorable – in a good way – and stands in sharp contrast to other check-ins I've experienced (and ones you've had too).

So let's look at how this same scenario might play out with an employee who was not being his authentic self.

Again, I'm arriving at 1:00 am on a rainy night, pulling a suitcase behind me.

Front desk person: "Hello, and welcome to XYZ Hotel! Are you checking in?"

Although I might be polite, what I'd be thinking is this: "No, I'm selling Fuller Brushes at 1:00 in the morning. That's what's in my suitcase! Would you like to buy some? *Of course I'm checking in,* you robot!"

Or the front desk person might say: "Hello, and welcome to XYZ Hotel! How are you today?"

I'd likely mutter "OK" but I'd be thinking, "It's 1:00 am, and I'm clearly soaking wet. I'm *miserable*, that's how I am!"

Next, the front desk person might say, "Mr. Magenta, we appreciate your loyalty! I see you have forty zillion points in our loyalty program. Thank you!"

Again, I'd mumble or nod, but I'd be fuming inside, thinking, "This is not the time for this! Don't tell me the stats and thank me *now*. Just get me into my room!"

You probably know what comes next – the front desk person explains the amenities. He cheerfully says, "Breakfast is in the Garden Room, the pool is open until 10, and we have a complimentary reception each evening at 6 pm."

But he already noted that I'm a loyal customer and I stay here often, so I probably know all this by heart. I'd want to say, "Stop already, and just let me get some rest!"

Now…bear in mind that this employee's actions would have been *exactly* in keeping with the protocol of many hospitality companies! I would have been greeted as scripted, thanked for my loyalty, and had the amenities explained, all in proper order. But for me, in that situation, it would have meant nothing! I wouldn't remember any of it, except that I would have felt annoyed and processed, not welcomed. This would hardly have been a great customer experience.

Both of these experiences upheld brand standards, yet only one was authentic and therefore memorable. Only one created a differentiated customer experience. By the way, which employee do you think was more engaged?

So when we invest in our frontline employees to ensure they understand the brand they represent and the products and services of that brand, and we empower them to bring their authentic selves to their job, who wins? Everybody.

- Customers win because they feel as if they're in a relationship (and they are).
- Employees win because they aren't play-acting, but bringing their authentic selves to work every day.
- And the organization wins by gaining the loyalty of both customers and employees.

An engaged employee who is happy because he understands his job and has the freedom to be himself spreads this feeling to customers – it's called "emotional contagion." Marketing guru, Thorsten Hennig-Thurau writes, "The theory of emotional contagion holds that when a service employee is happy, this will be contagious and literally infect the emotional condition of the customer."[1]

If you truly believe the customer experience will never exceed the employee experience, hire the right personality to fit your brand – whether your brand is irreverent or formal — invest in training them, and encourage them to be authentic. Then watch your employees deliver those memorable customer experiences.

[1] Thorsten Hennig-Thurau, Markus Groth, Michael Paul, and Dwayne D. Gremler (2006) "Are All Smiles Created Equal? How Emotional Contagion and Emotional Labor Affect Service Relationships." Journal of Marketing, 70(3), pp. 58-73.

TRY THIS

- Hire personalities that match your business's personality.
- Encourage your employees to build relationships with each other and with customers – maybe highlight stories of great customer experiences being delivered by your team as a part of the daily practices.
- Encourage your employees to deliver the customer experience in a way that lets their passion shine through while still upholding brand standards.
- Allow your frontline to be themselves and give them a great manager who brings out their best.

NOTES

NOTES

Chapter 10
Starting with the End in Mind:
Imagine Your Most Loyal Customers

"You need to have people really connect to 'How do I fit? How do I carry out this commitment that we have to our customers?' "

— Charlie Piscitello, *Chief People Officer of Petco*

When the customer experience breaks down, whose fault is it?

Don't answer until you read this story a friend recently told me. Her home Internet and cable connections broke down, so she called her provider, Comcast, and this is how the next few days unfolded:

- **Day 1.** She talked to a Customer Service Representative (CSR) who tried to resolve the issue over the phone. After many transfers, her Internet was restored, but not the cable.
- **Day 2.** She called again and explained her problem to a different CSR. This time, the cable service returned, but the Internet disappeared.
- **Day 3.** Both the cable and the Internet quit. Irritated, she called again, and the company scheduled a technician to come to her house the next day.
- **Day 4.** She waited during a multi-hour window for the tech to show up. He did not. Totally aggravated, she again called the company. This CSR apologized, offered to reschedule the appointment, and assured her that he would credit her $20 to make up for her trouble (as if that made everything better).

At this point, her patience totally exhausted, she said to the CSR, "I have to tell you – I've been dealing with this for four days with no resolution. *I hate Comcast.*" To which the CSR replied, "I hate Comcast too, but at least you don't have to work here."

No business wants this to happen. When a customer is dissatisfied and wants to share her frustration, she usually finds validation with a friend who's had the same experience – that "I've been there too" response. But when a customer is as exasperated as my friend in this story, the *last* person who should echo her response should be an *employee!*

So whose fault was it that this customer experience broke down? If your first instinct was to fire that CSR, hold on. *It's not his fault.*

What this story really highlights is the importance of an underlying customer first culture that includes everyone from top leadership to frontline employees. Here, there was no customer first culture. No one who talked to my friend was empowered to deliver a great customer experience. Where was the manager in this situation? Why wasn't the CSR trained in delivering the best customer experience? Whether he knew it or not, the CSR was frustrated that he wasn't empowered to act authentically, and he found an outlet for that frustration in this phone call.

When the customer experience is delivered well, it's because it begins with insights directly from customers. Using those insights, the culture is designed by leaders and flows from empowered managers who train frontline employees to deliver it authentically.

To see how this works in the real world, let's look at a different story – about a company that started a journey by envisioning the experience their customers wanted to have, and then determining the changes that were needed for leaders, managers, and frontliners to bring that experience to life.

The Petco Journey - A Client Case Study

Baby Boomers, Gen Xers, Millennials – they all have their unique eccentricities, but they have one thing in common: they love their animals. As a Boomer, I'll admit that the dog has now become a prominent figure in my empty nest. Across generations, the humanization of animals is a common trend. Have you seen a dog in a stroller in your neighborhood? I have. I remember the first time I peeked into a baby carriage to be greeted by a baby pug – a face only a mother could love.

Tapping into this pet-as-family-member trend was important to Petco, a company that's been revolutionizing the pet supply business since 1965. In its more than 1,400 locations in the United States, Mexico, and Puerto Rico, Petco has been touting its "Think Adoption First" philosophy long before it was popular, encouraging adoption over purchase whenever possible. The company's innovative thinking doesn't stop there. A leader in supplies, nutrition, and even pet advocacy by the early 2000s, Petco's leaders set their sights on taking customer loyalty to a new level. They knew they couldn't rely on just product differentiation – loyalty would have to come from creating a differentiated customer experience.

To create that, Petco's executive team had to be willing to take an honest look in the mirror. The team needed a clear picture of the changing marketplace around them. It needed to see how customers thought about the organization at an emotional level and how customers compared Petco to competitors. Petco leadership had to dig deep to understand changing customer needs so they could create an experience based on *exceeding* those needs, including offering products and services that customers didn't even know they wanted yet.

Petco leaders knew they couldn't take this journey alone. They needed to engage the whole organization.

Petco leaders were really smart; they knew they couldn't take this journey alone. They had to engage the entire organization.

- They would need to *align their leaders* on the brand, strategy, actions, and behaviors required to create a differentiated customer experience – they needed a new culture, one that resulted in driving greater associate and customer loyalty.

- They wanted *managers to be "ambassadors of change,"* acting as a conduit between the strategy and employees, empowered to act like owners in all 1,400 Petco locations.
- They would have to *engage their employees* in the "why, what, and how" of delivering a differentiated customer experience, one that turned customers into fans through every action and interaction, in every store, every time.

So with the vision and strategy set for the future, and the knowledge that the company would need strong managers to lead the desired customer experience, Petco began the arduous task of transforming its managers into great leaders.

Petco realized that its highest-performing stores were led by managers who were innately great leaders – instinctively gifted when it came to engaging their employees. These innately great managers knew that, first and foremost, their role was that of "CEO" – Chief *Engagement* Officer – for their employees. They knew that they were Petco's representatives in their stores, that their employees saw Petco as a company through their eyes. And they could consistently show each employee how his or her individual work supported the greater goals of the company.

The average managers knew the basics about their customers, competitors, merchandise, and employees, but the innately great managers knew more, like:
- How to connect their teams to the marketplace
- How to coach their employees
- How to set clear performance expectations
- How to follow up to ensure the best results

These managers who represented the "best in class" needed to be replicated. Petco meticulously and methodically studied the distinctive skills of these managers and worked to build them with every store manager across the organization. With a strategy in place and managers who were prepared to lead, they could now engage the frontline in delivering a new customer experience.

Leaders were aligned on the strategy and managers had the skills to lead before they engaged the frontline.

Many organizations make the mistake of starting with frontline training when they set out to improve the customer experience. But Petco did it the right way. They first made sure their leaders were aligned on the strategy and their managers had the skills to lead *before* they engaged the frontline.

Frontline training included understanding the "big picture" of the marketplace and Petco's strategy for success. The company brought employees into the story so each person could see how they fit in. Training included simulations and games that matched the demographics of the frontline, connecting employees' passion for pets to the Petco brand, and connecting their passion and the brand to the customer experience.

So what were the results? Once leaders were aligned, managers were empowered, and the frontline was engaged, the results were powerful. Manager effectiveness rose by 8%. There was a rise in employee engagement of 9%. The ultimate prize was an increase in customer loyalty of 10%. And the major bonus? Employee turnover decreased by a whopping 35%.

Manager effectiveness up **8%**

Employee engagement up from **75** to **84%**

Customer loyalty index up from **70** to **80%**

Turnover down **35%**

Unprecedented performance (recession)

What's unique about Petco is that it didn't start its quest for loyal customers by working with the frontline, as most businesses do. The company needed, wanted, and was willing to put in the work to create a holistic and sustainable change in the business. It took the time and necessary steps to engage leaders, managers, and the frontline to deliver a customer experience that resulted in a meaningful change in customer loyalty scores.

As a leader in your business, you have this same opportunity to create meaningful change. It starts by resisting the notion that, to change the frontline customer experience, you must start by training frontline employees. It starts at the top. It starts with you.

Note: During the writing of this book, CVC Capital Partners and the Canada Pension Plan Investment Board agreed to acquire Petco.

NOTES

NOTES

720 Haircuts

If you want loyal customers in today's customer experience economy, you must create a true, honest, and enduring emotional connection to your brand. *You have to make your customers fall in love with you.*

Throughout the years, customers have had different motivators for being loyal. Selection, quality, service, relationships, product, price, guarantees, warranties – these have all been key determinants of loyalty. But today, all of these things are easily replicable. Customer experience is the "final frontier" because *it's the only thing you offer that cannot be and never will be replicated.* It is your organization's fingerprint, unique to you alone. The customer experience is a mindset, a culture. It exists in every thought, act, and behavior. Defining and delivering it requires everyone to be involved, whether or not they ever interact with a customer. Leadership, management, and the frontline all have important roles in delivering the customer experience.

Where does the responsibility lie for initiating this customer experience? If you're the leader of your business, look in the mirror – customer experience starts with you. If you're an influencer in your business, this is the time to engage your leadership to take ownership in creating the kind of experience that drives loyalty.

If you want to create an experience that has customers banging on your door (or banging on their computer keys) to give you their hearts and a portion of their wallets, ask yourself these questions:

- *Are your leaders aligned on a customer experience strategy,* and are they committed to it?
- *Are your managers empowered to act like owners* and make decisions specific to their areas of the business?
- *Does everyone understand the marketplace* – the competition, the customers, economics, threats, and opportunities?
- *Does the frontline have the skills and knowledge* to deliver the customer experience authentically?

I'll close with a story that illustrates the beauty of a great customer experience that grew from a single moment into a lifetime of loyalty.

720 haircuts, and counting...

Uncle Mel and Charlie the Barber

In the 1950s, my Uncle Mel was growing up in northern New Jersey. He was 14 and a high school student in search of a haircut when he first walked into Charles Hair Specialists. The owner cut his hair, and Mel liked it. He came back the next month, and kept coming back. He liked his haircut as well as the ambience of the place – the way the people in the shop made him feel.

In a few years, the owner's son, Charlie, took over the business, although his dad remained a fixture in the shop. Charlie was just a few years older than Mel, and they became friends, talking about sports, things going on in town, and probably girls. There were lots of barbershops in the area, but Mel chose this shop because he felt an emotional connection to the experience, and to Charlie himself.

Mel went on to college, got married, had three children, and went to graduate school. But through it all, he was at Charles Hair Specialists every month for his haircut. The people who cut his hair changed now and then, but he always returned to the same shop. Charlie remained a barber throughout his life, while Mel earned a PhD in chemical engineering, held 18 U.S. patents in plastics, and worked for Fortune 500 companies in the New York metropolitan area. He was often as far as 100 miles from the shop, and could have had his hair cut at any number of places that were far more convenient.

But he never did. Every month without fail, my Uncle Mel has made that trip to Charles Hair Specialists for his haircut. *For more than 60 years, he never missed a single month,* no matter where he lived. The barbershop has moved several times and multiple people have cut Uncle Mel's hair. Over more than half a century, price, convenience, competitors, and trends have changed and evolved, but that loyalty – dare I say love – has kept my uncle going back to Charlie's for more than *720 haircuts.*

Today, Uncle Mel is 74 years old, and he drives 57 miles each way from his house to the shop every month. And for the same reasons. Here's what Uncle Mel told me as I was writing this book:

> "They care about me. They're interested in me, and they know what I like. They know the sports teams I root for, and how I like to have my hair washed. We've become friends and confidantes. They created an environment where I feel welcomed, and I'm like a member of their family. I have a relationship with every member of their team."

Over the years, the shop's ownership was passed down through the family. Charlie inherited the store from his father, Charles, and then Charlie's son, Chuck, followed in the family footsteps. Today, Carol, a non-family employee, cuts my uncle's hair. Although Charlie is 82 and retired, he still comes to the store to visit with his longtime clients. As Uncle Mel says, the experience is mostly about the feeling – the connection to the store and its people – that makes customers come back for decades.

You see, it's not really about the haircut. It never is.